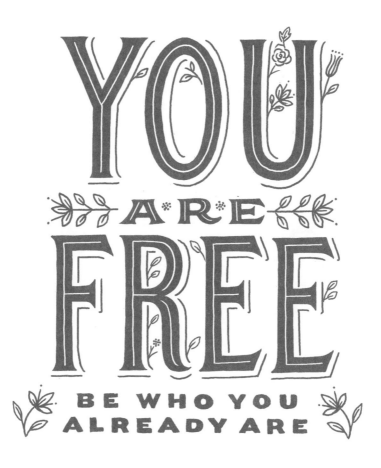

YOU ARE FREE

BE WHO YOU ALREADY ARE

STUDY GUIDE
SIX SESSIONS

REBEKAH LYONS

& ANNIE F. DOWNS

ZONDERVAN

© 2017 by Rebekah Lyons

This title is also available as a Zondervan ebook.

Requests for information should be addressed to:
Zondervan, *3900 Sparks Dr. SE, Grand Rapids, Michigan 49546*

ISBN 978-0-310-08561-4

Rebekah Lyons is represented by Christopher Ferebee, Attorney and Literary Agent, www.christopherferebee.com.

Annie F. Downs is represented by Alive Literary Agency, 7680 Goddard Street, Suite 200, Colorado Springs, Colorado 80920, www.aliveliteraryagency.com.

Cover illustration: Dana Tanamachi
Interior design: Kait Lamphere

First Printing December 2016 / Printed in the United States of America

Contents

Introduction

WHEN WE LOOK AT the pages of Scripture, it's clear that God intends for us to "live as free people" (1 Peter 2:16). We are assured that "where the Spirit of the Lord is, there is freedom" (2 Corinthians 3:17) and that "it is for freedom that Christ has set us free" (Galatians 5:1). Furthermore, Jesus declared a "kingdom come"—a kingdom of complete freedom—"on earth as it is in heaven" (Matthew 6:10), and Paul teaches this kingdom power lives in us (see Romans 8:11). This means that even in our feeble weakness, if we claim Christ and his resurrection, somehow we are God's agents who carry freedom to the world.

So, given all these passages in the Bible, why don't we see this kind of kingdom-come freedom more? Why do we hobble through our days, longing for the God who promises life "to the full" (John 10:10), but failing to truly experience this type of kingdom power in our lives? We want to see the Jesus who calms the storm, frees the oppressed, heals the sick, and raises the dead (see Luke 8:22–56). Yet here we are, living our lives one small step at a time, feeling so powerless to loosen the chains that bind us, let alone helping others live in freedom.

I know this struggle all too well. All my life I ran the hamster wheel of achievement and acceptance. As a child, I earned love by working hard to fit in. At church, I earned love by memorizing verses. At school, I earned love by pleasing teachers. The God I was striving for was rigid and lifeless and seemed far away. Although I believed he was real, I wasn't convinced he was good. So I went on trying to be the best version of myself, hoping maybe I'd catch a glimpse of his approval. Legalism shaped me, driving my performance.

If someone had asked me in my youth why I was doing all this striving, I wouldn't have had an answer. It took decades for me to peel back the layers of bondage and realize that freedom only comes *when we know God is enough—when he is our everything.* When he is our peace and our strength, joy, and rest. Our provision, healer, hope, fortress, shelter, strong tower, and Father. Freedom reveals everything good is from him and by him and for him. Every breath we take, every person we encounter, every word we utter is all an expression of a freedom where God dwells in us and loves through us!

In this study, I want to walk you through my journey into this kind of freedom and explore what the Bible says true freedom looks like for our lives. We will wrestle through tough realities, and I will ask questions—some easy to answer and others painful. My only request is that you leave nothing on the table. No stone unturned, no whispers unspoken, no secret still hidden. This freedom thing is costly but worth it.

Freedom is for everyone who wants it—the lost, the wounded, and those weary from all of the striving. It's for those who gave up trying years ago. It's for professional Christians hiding secrets. It's for the angry and hurt. I write for you, for all of you. You are the church, the people of God. You were meant to be free.

Will you join in this freedom journey with me?

—REBEKAH LYONS

How to Use This Guide

$\mathcal{T}$HE *YOU ARE FREE* study is designed to be experienced in a group setting such as a Bible study, Sunday school class, or any small-group gathering. Each session begins with a brief introduction followed by "icebreaker" questions to get you interacting with the others in your group. You will then watch the video with Rebekah Lyons and jump into some directed small-group discussion. Note that even though there are multiple questions available for discussion, don't feel that you have to use them all. Your leader will focus on the ones that resonate most with your group and guide you from there.

Each session will conclude with an individual activity and closing prayer. For the activity, you and your group will engage in some hands-on practical exercises that will help you move the content of the session from your head to your heart. Think of this time as an answer to the question, "What am I supposed to *do* with this message?"

Note that this study will be what you make of it. If you choose to just go through the motions, or if you refrain from participating, there is less chance you will find what you're looking for during this study. But if you stay open to what God is saying to you and are willing to take a gamble, you may discover what so many others have already found to be true: faith and freedom come alive when we take holy risks for God.

Following your group time, you will have several more opportunities to engage the content of *You Are Free* during the week. The first of these "between-sessions" activities is designed to help you *reflect* on the content of the session and apply it more personally to your life. The second portion will help you examine your life, open your heart to God, and *confess* any areas that are keeping you from experiencing the freedom that he has for you. The final portion will enable you to *respond* to the message through guided journaling and prayer activities.

Beginning in session two, there will be time in your group meeting before the video to check in about the previous week's activity and process your experiences as a group. Don't worry if you are unable to do an activity one week or are just joining the study. It will still be beneficial for you to hear from the other participants in the group and learn about what they discovered during the week.

Remember that the real growth in this study will happen during your small-group time. This is where you will process the content of the message, ask questions, and learn from others as you listen to what God is doing in their lives. As you go through this study, keep in mind that the videos, discussions, and activities are simply meant to kick-start your imagination so you are not only open to what God wants you to hear but also how to apply that to your life.

So, are you ready to experience the true freedom, peace, and joy that only Jesus can bring? Then let's jump into *You Are Free*!

Note

If you are a group leader, additional instructions and resources are found in the back of this guide to help you lead your members through the study. Because some of the activities require materials and set up, make sure you read this content so you will be prepared.

To Be Free

We compete, and we compare, and we strive, and we put terrible pressure on ourselves to "keep up." But the good news is that we were not made to keep up. We were made to be free . . . to be who we already are.

REBEKAH LYONS

INTRODUCTION

Country music superstar Garth Brooks and Christian recording artist Susan Ashton recorded the same song about twenty years ago called "You Move Me." The lyrics to the chorus read in part:

You give me courage I didn't know I had . . .
Now I can't go with you and stay where I am,
So you move me.

Garth's version played on the radio this morning, and as I (Annie) sat here at my computer, tears began to form in my eyes. I was singing along, the words coming right back to the front of my mind even though I hadn't heard the song in probably more than a decade. I knew Susan Ashton's version first, so I can't listen to it and not think of it as a prayer I'm singing to God.

As we embark on this journey of freedom together, the question is: are those lyrics among the prayers in your heart to God?

Freedom is just that: we can't go with God into a free place and stay where we are. But thankfully, he moves us. For me, it was a literal city move to Nashville, Tennessee. I didn't know at the time that it was a move of freedom, an invitation to walk toward a freer life, but it always was. God always knew.

He knew my heart like he knows yours. He knew I wanted to go with him, wherever that led. And that's why you're here too, right? Because you want what he wants for you—and that, my friend, is freedom.

I think freedom in Christ is less like a tightrope we are meant to carefully balance our way across and more like a wide river that we get to jump in and float down. God moves us. We may plant and we may harvest, but he is the One who grows. He is the One who calls. He is the One who makes us brave enough to face old sin patterns and worries and leave them on the riverbank.

Freedom isn't a tricky thing. It is truly and purely freedom. If you want to be free in Christ, you can. Let's learn how.

WELCOME

Welcome to the first session of You Are Free: Be Who You Already Are. *If you or any of your fellow group members do not know one another, take a little time to introduce yourself. Next, to get things started, discuss either of the following questions:*

- What made you decide to participate in this study?
- What does freedom mean to you?

VIDEO PRESENTATION

Play the video segment for session one. As you watch, use the following outline to record any thoughts or concepts that stand out to you.

Notes

Over time, the fear and approval of men and women can get louder than our intimacy and union with God.

We want to please God and love him, but it's easy to fall into the trap of shifting our gaze to men and women—and wanting to please *them*.

"Let us throw off everything that hinders and the sin that so easily entangles. And let us run with perseverance the race marked out for us" (Hebrews 12:1). Burden and bondage are like dead weight on a runner that's limping across the finish line.

Paul writes, "Do not let yourselves be burdened again by a yoke of slavery" (Galatians 5:1). Often we want communion with God, but we also want to hold onto our yoke of slavery.

Meaning follows surrender. When we fully surrender ourselves and our lives to Jesus, he fills us with his higher purpose.

Our calling and purpose—the assignment that God has for us—is often informed by the thing that breaks our heart and causes us pain.

Calling is where our talents and our burdens collide.

If we are able to admit our losses in life, we will be able to reclaim the gifts we once possessed.

GROUP DISCUSSION

Take a few minutes with your group members to discuss what you just watched and explore these concepts in Scripture.

1. What's a favorite childhood memory of freedom for you? (Rebekah shared about riding her bicycle.)

2. How would you explain the idea that "meaning follows surrender"? How have you seen that truth play out in your life?

3. In what ways do you struggle with being a people pleaser?

4. Read **Galatians 5:1**. What does this verse mean to you personally when you think about freedom in Christ?

5. How do you see your burdens and your talents colliding in your life right now?

6. In what ways have you seen purpose come from pain in your life or the lives of the people around you? What did that process look like?

7. Read **2 Corinthians 3:17**. How do freedom and calling go together? Give a personal example if you can think of one.

8. Author and educator Parker Palmer says, "We arrive in this world with birthright gifts—then we spend the first half of our lives abandoning them or letting others disabuse us of them." In what ways have you found this to be true in your life?

INDIVIDUAL ACTIVITY

For this activity, each participant will need a note card.

As you close this session, answer the following question on a note card: "What do you hope to learn and experience in this study?" On the other side of the card, answer this question: "When you think about your calling, what comes to mind?"

CLOSING PRAYER

Ask the women in the group to read aloud the first answer from their note card—what they hope to gain from this study. Take time together to pray for those requests. Ask that God would show up for each woman as she needs and that she would see him moving in a unique way to her heart and calling.

RECOMMENDED READING

As you reflect on what God is teaching you through this session, review chapters 1–3 of the book *You Are Free* by Rebekah Lyons. In preparation for your next session, read chapters 4–6.

Between-Sessions Personal Study

SESSION 1

*Y*OU ARE INVITED TO further explore the material you've covered this week by engaging in any or all of the following between-sessions activities. *Be sure to read the reflection questions after each activity and make a few notes in your guide about the experience.* There will be a time for you to share these reflections at the beginning of the next session.

REFLECT

I (Annie) was with a friend at a local Nashville restaurant, and I couldn't decide what to have for dinner. The waiter stopped by a few times to take our order, but I couldn't make up my mind. Turkey burger with sweet potato fries? Or a kale salad with truffle oil fries? Two of my favorite meals in Nashville. I just couldn't narrow it down.

As the waiter made his third pass, I looked at my friend and said, "I don't know what I want. You just order for me."

(The turkey burger was a great choice. I appreciated her quick decision making.)

About a week or so later, I was walking through the mall and passed a discount shoe store. One of those, you know, with hundreds of pairs of shoes lined up and down shelves. In the window display I noticed a pair of camel-colored mid-calf boots.

I walked into the store, and the woman behind the counter said, "Can I help you?"

I pointed directly at the window display and said, "THOSE. Those camel boots. I want those." And the woman led me to the right aisle.

Decision making isn't hard for me when I know what I want. But isn't that usually the case? When you know *exactly* what you want—as I knew with those beautiful boots (which I am wearing right now)—you just say it.

So . . . what is it that *you* want? Deep down.

Read **Matthew 20:29–34**. How would you describe the scene (verses 29–30)?

What does Jesus ask the two men (verse 32)?

It seems like the answer would be obvious to the men, doesn't it? They aren't deciding between great options on a menu. There is one clear thing they need: sight. And yet, Jesus asks them what they want him to do for them.

Why do you think Jesus did this?

Jesus wants to hear your desires. It's like the waiter who asked me and my friend what food we wanted, because he wanted to bring us just what would satisfy. The woman at the shoe store was the same—she wanted me to have exactly what I wanted. That's why she asked.

Jesus wants to hear your desires, hear your wants, even though he can clearly see what you need. And when it comes to freedom, he wants to give it to you.

You *can* be free. You may feel that you will be bound forever, or that you will be trapped forever, but you won't. Jesus brings freedom, and he brings it just so you'll be free.

Read **Galatians 5:1** again. What is Jesus' purpose in setting you free?

Jesus' purpose is not just for his glory (though it is). It's not just as a witness to the people around you (though it is). It's not to make you indebted to him (though you are). It's just for freedom. Because he doesn't want you to be bound. That's why he offers freedom: so you can leave a life of slavery, pursue your calling, and live free.

"From the beginning of time, all God ever wanted was our union with him. He didn't create Adam and Eve because he wanted help cultivating the earth or naming the animals. Believe me, God is capable of this all by himself! No, he created man and woman because he wanted companionship. They were the pinnacles of his creation. He delighted in them and wanted intimacy with them. His purpose for them—and us—was freedom to walk with him."

YOU ARE FREE, PAGE 28

CONFESS

We are going to dig deeper into confession during our next session, as it is truly at the center of entering into freedom in Christ. Opening your heart to God—being willing to admit your faults and rough spots and to look at your pain, history, shame, and sins—is the step toward healthy confession that allows God to heal you and set you free.

Read **2 Corinthians 3:17** and fill in the blanks: "Where the <u>Spirit of the Lord</u> is, there is <u>freedom</u>."

Here's what we know: where the Spirit of the Lord is, there is freedom. So, as you pray and confess today, start by thanking God that wherever he is, there is freedom.

Confess the ways you have . . .
- Compared yourself to others

  All the time - people are smarter
  deeper thinkers
  better instructors
  better Christians
  have all their crap together

- Strived to be someone you aren't

- Chosen bondage over freedom because it felt easier

Confess, either in written word here or out loud with your mouth, that yes, you can be free. YOU CAN BE FREE!

On the line below, write "I can be free."

_____

If you are feeling brave today (and I hope you are!), on the next line write "I can be free of . . ." (and mention something you feel has been holding you back).

_____

"Many of us in the church operate from a place of wounding. Some hide their wounds in shame. Others aim to prove themselves worthy. Many seek the approval of others; they take pride in the work of their hands. Consequently, we have created a culture of inadequacy and comparison in the body of Christ, causing many believers to feel a terrible pressure to strive. I wonder if Jesus looks at all our posturing, and says, 'I didn't ask you to do that.'"

YOU ARE FREE, PAGE 30

RESPOND

Do you have a journal? If not, you may want one before this study is over. This doesn't have to be fancy—just some sort of notebook from your local bookstore or even the school supply section of your grocery. It will be helpful as you process, learn, and grow through this season. If you do not have a journal, use the lines below to answer the following questions:

Write

In what areas of your life do you feel bound?

What five words describe freedom to you?

1. _____
2. _____
3. _____
4. _____
5. _____

How would freedom change your life?

What would be different about tomorrow if you believed that you could be free?

If Jesus were standing right in front of you, and he asked you the same question that he asked the two blind men in Matthew 20:29–34, how would you answer? What do you want him to do for you?

Act

Take a walk around your house or your neighborhood, or head out on a hike. Put a little music in your ears and as your feet move you forward, think, and maybe pray. But definitely think. What is this study about for you? What scares you about this study? What are your hopes? Expectations? What does freedom mean for you? Take some time, here at the start, to connect with your heart and ask some important questions. If you'd like, jot down your thoughts here.

Pray

You. Can. Be. Free. Read the prayer below or copy it in your journal. Add your own thoughts, experiences, and emotions as you write.

Dear God, I want to be free. I know I do. In all the ways I can identify and in all the ways I can't quite see yet, I want freedom. In the areas where I feel bound to sin, I want freedom. In the mind-sets from my past, I want freedom. In the places of pain that I always return to, I want freedom. Meet me in this study time, in these pages, as I watch the videos and interact with my small group. Change me from the inside out. My eyes are open to what you are doing here in my life and in the areas of confession, healing, and freedom. I'm looking to you for freedom. I want to be free, and I believe that with you, only you, I can be free.

Free to Confess

Darkness cannot drive out darkness; only light can do that.
Hate cannot drive out hate; only love can do that.
MARTIN LUTHER KING JR.

INTRODUCTION

When kids are small, the dark of night can be so scary. I (Annie) kept a flashlight beside my bed for most of my childhood, using it often to read under my covers on the nights my parents told me, for the tenth time, to turn off my bedside light and go to sleep. It was often *Nancy Drew*. I read every one of them. I could barely get to the last page of one before I picked up the next. I craved reading until the end of the chapter—and then, okay, ONE MORE CHAPTER. More often than not, I fell asleep with my glasses still on my face, my book sprawled open beside me, and my flashlight still illuminated.

But there were other times when the flashlight was a different kind of gift in the darkness. In the moments when fear whispered that I was alone, or that I was surrounded by monsters and goblins, one quick grab of the flashlight brought freedom and peace to my troubled little heart. I would muster up all the courage I could find, hang my head below my four-poster bed, and blaze that flashlight beam beneath it. Nope, nothing there. I was safe. The light proved it.

Confession is like that flashlight that brightens a dark space. We often let shame keep us hidden in the darkness, away from any form of light, away from the freedom we crave. But once we get brave—once we are willing to face the darkness with the Light in our hands—peace comes. Quiet comes. The power shifts from the darkness to the Light.

In this session, we will dig deeply into the power of confession. When combined with declaration, confession becomes more than a simple tool toward forgiveness. Our prayers deepen in effectiveness, our heart draws nearer to God, and the light shines in the darkness when we take our full selves before Jesus—flaws and all.

WELCOME

Welcome to the second session of You Are Free: Be Who You Already Are. *To get things started, go around the group and discuss any one of the following questions:*

- What insights do you have to share with the group from the between-sessions study last week?
- What new thoughts or ideas do you have about your *calling*? About where your burdens and your gifts meet?
- When you think about *confession*, what words or pictures come to your mind?

VIDEO PRESENTATION

Play the video segment for session two. As you watch, use the following outline to record any thoughts or concepts that stand out to you.

Notes

"Those who keep score in life just want to know that they count, but when you do what you do for an audience of one, you always know that you count." —Ann Voskamp

It is not enough to just know our birthright gifts and the burdens that break our heart and put our best foot forward to walk out a calling. If we're trying to do it in our own strength instead of the Lord's, it just becomes a prettier version of striving.

Confession is the gateway to freedom.

Confession begins with *repentance* and ends with *declaration*.

Declaration means we have a rightful authority and inheritance as daughters—and we can say so in our conversations with God.

Just like with the woman at the well in John 4:1–42, our *confession*, *declaration*, and the *revelation* of who Jesus is in our lives brings transformation to who we are.

Jesus wants to set us free to confess, to thirst, and to ask for more in our lives.

God does the miracle work. We are just responsible for asking.

Even when we feel weak in faith to ask God for something, all we have to do is approach him. He will do what only he can do in our situation.

GROUP DISCUSSION

Take a few minutes with your group members to discuss what you just watched and explore these concepts in Scripture.

1. Why do you think people are sometimes hesitant to confess their sins?

2. How have you seen confession open up your relationship with God? Briefly describe one such situation.

3. Read **Romans 8:1–2**. What does it mean that the "law of the Spirit who gives life" sets you free from the "law of sin and death"?

4. Why do we need to declare the truth about Jesus to ourselves before we declare him to other people? What tends to happen when we get the order backward?

5. How have you seen confession + declaration play out in your life?

6. Do you believe in miracles—the things that only God can do? If so, how have you experienced them in your life or the lives of people close to you? If you don't believe in miracles, what keeps you from believing?

7. Read **James 5:13–16**. What does this Scripture teach about the power of prayer?

8. What does this same passage teach about the importance of confession and declaration? Can you offer a firsthand example of this scriptural principle?

INDIVIDUAL ACTIVITY

As you read in James 5:16, there is power in confessing your sins to one another. So to close this session, partner up with someone in your group and share something difficult you currently are going through, or a sinful pattern that has been a struggle for you lately. Be brave, willingly sharing what is going on in your life.

CLOSING PRAYER

James 5:16 also says that the prayer of a righteous man (or woman!) is powerful and effective. So pray with the woman who has shared her confession with you, and ask God to do his miracle work in your lives.

RECOMMENDED READING

As you reflect on what God is teaching you through this session, review chapters 4–6 of the book *You Are Free* by Rebekah Lyons. In preparation for your next session, read chapters 7–8.

Between-Sessions Personal Study

SESSION 2

YOU ARE INVITED TO further explore the material you've covered this week by engaging in any or all of the following between-sessions activities. *Be sure to read the reflection questions after each activity and make a few notes in your guide about the experience.* There will be a time for you to share these reflections at the beginning of the next session.

REFLECT

In John 4:1–42, we read a fascinating story about a conversation that Jesus had with a woman at a well. As the scene opens, Jesus is traveling from Judea to Galilee. There are a few different routes he could have taken on this journey north.

Using the map on the next page, draw a circle around Judea (where Jesus was at the start of this story) and Galilee (where he was headed). Put a box around Samaria, the land he had to pass through.

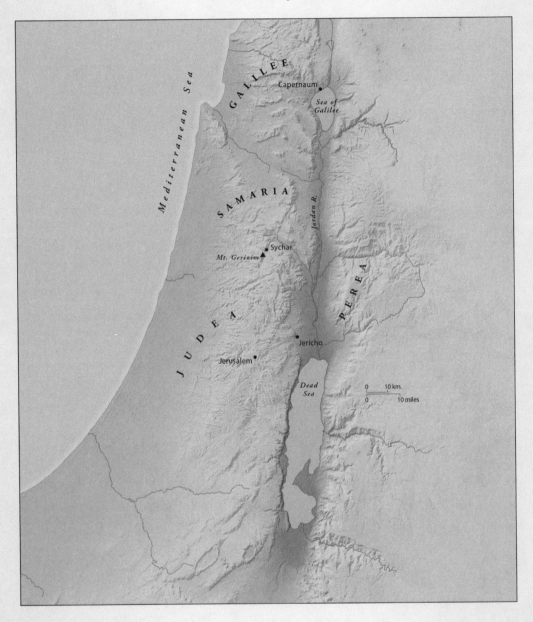

Why did Jesus go back to Galilee in the first place (see verses 1–3)?

What city did Jesus stop in on his way back to Galilee (see verse 5), and why? Put a star on the map beside this city.

I love the idea in verses 7–8 of Jesus waiting by the well at the edge of town as his disciples go into town to buy food. Jesus is just hanging out, thinking, sitting, resting. But be sure, friend, that he is there on purpose—and that purpose is to meet the Samaritan woman. This woman is full of confessions—the kind that take real courage and heart strength to say out loud. As you read, notice the different confessions she makes:

- Confessing her insecurities
- Confessing her confusion
- Confessing her need
- Confessing her sins

Which of the four confessions listed above does the woman make in verse 9?

Why do you think the woman calls out the difference between her religious upbringing and Jesus'?

The woman is showing her insecurities. She feels as if she isn't the "right" woman to be standing there having this conversation. Sometimes confession looks like that, doesn't it? You confess that you feel you don't fit in, with "them," in the life you have. There is power in giving your insecurities a voice and bringing them out of the darkness into the light.

When has sharing your insecurities with someone else led to healing for you?

When she asks for water in verse 10, the Samaritan woman confesses her confusion right there to the face of God's Son. *How is Jesus going to get water without a bucket? What is "living water"? Who is this person?* We've all done this before. We wonder why things aren't working out as we thought they should, or how God is going to fix a situation we find ourselves in, or who this God is and how he and we both ended up here.

Recall a time when you confessed your confusion to God. What answer did you receive?

In verse 15 the woman confesses her need: she desires the living water that comes from Jesus alone. What do you think Jesus meant by "living water"? Why does it matter that the woman confessed her need for a water that would quench her thirst?

We now come to the part of the story that is most familiar to those of us who have read or heard of the Samaritan woman. She confesses that she lives with a man who is not her husband and has sinned in her past. In these few verses (16–18), she allows Jesus to see her, *really* see her—her shame, past mistakes, and heartache. And Jesus doesn't walk away. He doesn't belittle her. He stands with her and continues to speak truth into her life.

What does it mean to you to know that Jesus won't walk away when you confess your sins to him?

What has kept you from confessing your sins to Christ in times past?

Remember that it's this combination of confession and declaration that leads to freedom. That's exactly what the Samaritan woman does next. Jump down to John 4:29. "Come," the woman says, "see a man who told me everything I ever did. Could this be the Christ?"

Could it? Could this be the Messiah, standing right there at the well, waiting on her to come out in the heat of the day, disconnected from her community, to hear her confessions and become her declaration? Yes. The Messiah has come, and he came straight to her. Right in her piles of confessions, right in the center of the place she went in her shame, right where freedom was waiting for her.

"Many of us are not free because we have not confessed the sins that hold us captive, keeping us in bondage. **Confession is the gateway to healing, the route to freedom.** *James teaches us this truth, writing, 'Confess your sins to each other and pray for each other so that you may be healed.'"*

YOU ARE FREE, PAGE 59

CONFESS

Start where the woman at the well started: by confessing your *insecurities*. Think up the memories, places, people, whispers, and the like that make you feel insecure so you can bring them right out in front of Jesus and allow him to deal with them.

Use the space below to write what you are struggling with right now—at work, at home, when you look in the mirror.

Are there any areas where you feel *confused*? Confess your confusion by making a list of the questions that you have for God right now.

Next, confess your *need*. Don't hesitate, don't be afraid; just ask. What do you need? Take some time to think about it, trusting that God is still standing there, right in front of you, hearing you, and will do something with all the questions and needs you have.

Now, let's shine some light into the darkness. Do you have *sins* to confess today? Something to bring to the Lord? A sin you have been struggling with and you need freedom from? Be brave enough to write it down here.

Let this only be the beginning. Invite Christ into your life through this discipline of confession and declaration each day. Your spiritual life will continue to deepen as you open your heart and mind to confessing and declaring that God is your strength, that Christ is your Savior, and that the Holy Spirit is your guide.

"Asking often requires an admission and confession of need, an acknowledgment that all is not well. Asking also requires us to do something, to participate in whatever God wants to do. We must initiate before God can respond. Finally, asking requires us to entrust what is beyond our control to the One who controls all. Asking awakens our holy imagination to God's divine intervention."

YOU ARE FREE, PAGE 89

RESPOND

Use the space provided or your journal to record your responses for this section.

Write

Rewrite each confession you made in the "Confess" section, and then write a Scripture that will declare truth over that confession. (If you need help finding verses, use biblegateway .com or a search engine like Google to look up verses that will bring truth into the situation.) For example, if your confession was that you need God to provide for your family financially, a good verse would be Philippians 4:19: "My God will meet all your needs according to the riches of his glory in Christ Jesus."

Act

Pull out a few note cards and write down some additional declarations about who Jesus is and how he will take care of you. (Use verses such as 1 Corinthians 8:6; Philippians 2:5–11; Hebrews 12:2; Hebrews 13:8; or 1 John 2:1.) Take the note cards and put these declared truths where you will see them each day—by the kitchen sink, on your bathroom mirror, on the dash of your car, or in the pocket of your purse. Freedom comes then, doesn't it? When your eyes are drawn to these words of truth about your life, bondage doesn't have quite the hold it once did.

Pray

Read the prayer below or copy it in your journal. Add your own thoughts, experiences, and emotions as you write.

Dear God, I feel a little drained, if I'm being honest, from all the confessing today. It feels a bit like I've been wrung out like a wet towel. But I'm here for freedom, and I want this discipline of confession and declaration to become a part of my daily life. Give me wisdom on how to do this well. Thank you for hearing me when I pray. Thank you, Jesus, that as I confess to you, you don't look away or walk away. Your kindness has led me to repentance, and I believe it will over and over and over again.

Free to Begin Again

If I find in myself desires which nothing in this world can satisfy,
the only logical explanation is that I was made for another world.
C. S. LEWIS

INTRODUCTION

Every time our (Annie's) family moves to a new house, I rethink just about everything. The vase on the dining room table in one house may not be the right vase for the next house. Or maybe it will go better on the bedside table in the guest room. Which kids should be in which rooms? What's the correct pairing? Should the television go on the main floor or upstairs? Three rugs, three rooms . . . which is right for which?

I'm an interior decorator at heart, so mixing around sofas and pieces of art, chairs and rugs, beds and lamps is really fun for me. (Of course, it may make my people a little crazy.)

As we've moved over the years, we've taken our pets, our clothes, our home décor, and furniture with us. Moving cities, moving spaces, and moving houses hasn't required me to get all new furniture or decorations. It's just forced me to rethink what we already have. I have kept my basic color palette—grays and whites with some hints of navy and yellow. But I've found the pieces that worked in one place (our multilevel house in Atlanta) didn't always work in another place (our two-bedroom apartment in New York or our tall skinny townhouse in Franklin).

And moving is always more work than I think it is going to be. It costs more money, requires more boxes, creates more trash, and takes up more time than I initially predict. But the newness, the fresh spaces, the opportunity to upgrade or downsize . . . it all works together to spark a new hope in what "home" really is or maybe could be this time.

New beginnings are like that. While they are not without their growing pains and problems, when God walks us (throws us?) into them, they are for our good, for our freedom, and for our peace. And I have found that God is continually pulling me toward himself, my truest home. For the most part, what I actually desire in the buildings where I live can't be found here. The deepest longings to begin again can only be satisfied in my connection to God himself.

And I find, over and over, as I begin again in homes, relationships, jobs, and experiences, that he is my true home.

WELCOME

Welcome to the third session of You Are Free: Be Who You Already Are. *To get things started, go around the group and discuss any one of the following questions:*

- What insights do you have to share with the group from the between-sessions study last week?
- Where are some of the cities and places you have lived? Which did you enjoy most?
- What's the best part about moving to a new house? What's the hardest part?

VIDEO PRESENTATION

Play the video segment for session three. As you watch, use the following outline to record any thoughts or concepts that stand out to you.

Notes

We are responsible for bringing our requests to God and asking him for what we want, need, and want to know. *Bringing our whole selves.*

"Interrupt my day... every day."

Confession and the freedom to declare who God is and who we are as his children will bring us new life.

"Beginning again" sounds exciting and optimistic, but there's a lot of fallout—emotional, spiritual, and professional—that comes with it.

Free to begin again. Transition is hard.
God says no matter where I am, he will be with me.
"Make your home in my arms — REST!" Home is not a place —
it is with God.

We never really know when God is going to ask us to begin again . . . and again . . . and again. So we have to keep our eyes and ears open for his voice.

When we are unsettled, we can lean on God more

John 14:23

We can always begin again when we know that God is our *true home*.

When we are untethered from what we have always known, and unsettled in a new place or season, it makes us hold onto God in faith and believe he will keep us.

We need to think about how we are ordering our lives around the person of Jesus. How is *he* becoming our shelter?

Time to hit the breaks a bit and rest with the Lord.

We cannot *see* the unknown until we *release* the known.

We hold on so tightly to the familiar.
be open to what He wants to show me.
In the waiting, God is working.
Do I trust Him?
Value in the resting and waiting

GROUP DISCUSSION

Take a few minutes with your group members to discuss what you just watched and explore these concepts in Scripture.

1. What is the relationship between confession and freedom? How has God used those two things together in your life?

2. In what ways can change be exciting? In what ways can it be painful? How can you hold onto both emotions at the same time?

3. Read **Psalm 139:7–10**. Describe a time when you had to begin again—either in a relationship or a job or another city. What do these verses say about God's presence during such times?

4. What does it look like to order your life around the person of Jesus?

5. Read **John 14:23**. Why does Jesus say that obedience to him connects us with his love? How does God make his home in us?

6. Beginning again means leaving the home you've known, either physically or emotionally or spiritually. How does making God your home affect your life? How does that truth play out in practical ways every day?

7. Why must we daily release the known for the unknown? How easy or difficult have you found this "letting go" to be? Share a brief story of how God has proven himself faithful when you let go.

8. How are you hiding in Jesus? How are you finding comfort and joy in him?

INDIVIDUAL ACTIVITY

For this activity, each participant will need a piece of paper with the simple outline of a house.

Take a few minutes to fill in the outline of the house with words that remind you of home. Discuss these words as a group and also ask how God can be each of those things to you.

CLOSING PRAYER

Spend time sharing requests about any new beginnings that group members are facing and then pray together about them.

RECOMMENDED READING

As you reflect on what God is teaching you through this session, review chapters 7–8 of the book *You Are Free* by Rebekah Lyons. In preparation for your next session, read chapters 9–10.

Between-Sessions Personal Study

SESSION 3

*Y*OU ARE INVITED TO further explore the material you've covered this week by engaging in any or all of the following between-sessions activities. *Be sure to read the reflection questions after each activity and make a few notes in your guide about the experience.* There will be a time for you to share these reflections at the beginning of the next session.

REFLECT

Midway through my (Annie's) fourth grade year, our county built a new elementary school. I had heard rumors that our neighborhood might get switched to the new school, but I hoped that wouldn't be the case. My mother had gone to the elementary school I was attending when she was a kid, and I wanted to spend my fifth-grade year in that building and finish up there as well. It was a beautiful old school, I knew my way around, and most of the teachers knew my family and me. *Please, please, please, let me stay at this school*, I thought.

I remember the day my fourth-grade teacher sent home letters with those of us who would be switching to the new school. I watched as she walked around the classroom, setting letters on random students' take-home folders. Then she came to me. I still remember the sad smile on her face as she handed me the envelope. The return address label was from the new school.

Even then, as a nine-year-old, I knew change wasn't easy and a new beginning was just around the corner. I teared up. Fear began to whisper to me about all the things I didn't know and all the people I wouldn't recognize and all the plans that would never come to pass. But my young mind also felt a quiet whisper from God. He had me. He was with me. Things were going to be okay.

As I recall this story, I think back to Abraham and the way he faced the freedom and fright of beginning again.

Read **Genesis 12:1–9**. What four things does God tell Abraham to do in verse 1?

1. Leave *your country*
2. Leave *your people*
3. Leave *your father's household*
4. Go to *the land I will show you*

In the next few verses, we find several responses we can have when God calls us into a new beginning.

Hold onto the Promises of God

What promises did God make to Abraham in Genesis 12:2–3?

① I will make you into a great nation
② I will bless you
③ I will make your name great
④ you will be a blessing.
⑤ I will bless those who bless you
⑥ I will curse whoever curses you
⑦ All peoples on the earth will be blessed through you

As Abraham was leaving his home and his people and going to somewhere foreign, this was the truth he had to carry with him.

Why does holding on to the promises of God during new beginnings matter?

because we can get scared, overwhelmed, doubtful and holding on to these promises helps me in the scary times.

When in your life have you had to hold on to the promises of God?

Every day that I have been writing in my journal about the promises of God. Claiming and remembering who I am in Christ.

Just like Abraham, we have to believe the promises of God are true and for us, even when we don't see them working out right away.

Remember You Don't Have to Go Alone

So often we feel isolated in new beginnings, as if no one else understands what we have left behind and the massive changes that are ahead of us. However, beginning again—whether at a job or in a church or in a relationship or in a living situation—gives us the opportunity to invite someone into the story with us. We don't have to go to the "new land" alone.

According to Genesis 12:4, who went into the new land with Abraham? How were the two related?

Lot went with him - nephew
Sarai - his wife - v.5

Isn't that interesting? Lot wasn't an older, wiser counselor—he was Abraham's younger nephew.

What might have been some of the reasons Abraham wanted Lot to join him in this new beginning?

How does having someone with you make beginning again easier?

Believe You Will Arrive

When Abraham, Sarah, Lot, and the others left Harran they did not really know where to go (Genesis 12:5); they just knew that God had called them to leave and head in the direction he was sending them. So much faith. And so much freedom.

On the days when the sand of the desert kicked up into their eyes or the tent flaps blew up in the night, this journey probably became less of an adventure and more of a challenge. Yet it is right there, in the moment when giving up seems like a great idea because this new life has gotten too hard, that we have to believe that someday we will arrive where God has promised we will go.

Where are you believing God that someday you will arrive? How is the journey going right now?

Keep Listening

As the group continued on their way, God spoke to Abraham again in Genesis 12:7.

Why do you think God chose to do this at this point?

Why do we often need a reminder that we are right where we are supposed to be?

How would such a reminder from God help you today?

Keep listening to God, keep turning your ear toward the Holy Spirit, and keep digging into the Scripture. In John 10:27, Jesus says the sheep will know the voice of their Shepherd. You can hear God for yourself. As you keep walking toward what is next, as you experience new beginnings again and again, his voice will be your guide.

Remember God

In Genesis 12:8–9, Abraham built an altar to the Lord and called on his name.

Abraham paused in his travels to remember God. Why is this important?

What did Abraham need to remember about God?

Not only was it important for Abraham to remember God's promises, his voice, and his character, he also needed a reminder—just as we still do today—that God was his true home. Making your home in God, ordering your life around Jesus (instead of your people or your home or your calling or your job), and finding true north in guidance from him, allows your temporary circumstances to shift and change while your faith remains unwavering. Each time you begin again—each time you draw near to God in the newness—your faith deepens, your prayers are more effective, and your heart is healed and set free.

"Sometimes it takes being stripped of what is familiar, giving everything up, to be reminded of who we truly are."

YOU ARE FREE, PAGE 99

CONFESS

As we continue to grow in our knowledge of God and long for the things of his heart, we continue to focus on confession and declaration as means to freedom in Christ. Abraham knew freedom. He pursued freedom for himself and his family, even when it was unknown, lonely, uncertain, and challenging.

Have there been times in your life when you knew the call to freedom, the call to step out of your comfort zone and into a new beginning, but you didn't want to go? If so, what happened?

In the space below, confess to God why it is sometimes scary to step into a new beginning. (If you are experiencing one now, you know the fear up close.)

What does it mean to make your home in God? What would that look like in your life right now?

Read **Isaiah 40:10–11**. How does this Scripture declare God's place in a new beginning? How does it speak to your heart today?

In the space below, write about who God is to you in transitions, when you are going from an ending to a new beginning, when you are walking toward more freedom.

RESPOND

In the space provided or in your journal, answer the following questions.

Write

Where in your life is God asking you to begin again?

What are some ways that beginning again—whether it is relationally, spiritually, professionally, or emotionally—could deepen your faith walk?

Write down some of the promises you feel that God has given you in this season.

Act

Walk around your house today (or your apartment, office space, or dorm room), and shift a few things. Maybe move a chair to a different room or throw away that burned-down candle and replace it with a fresh scent. Change up your surroundings a bit, and as you do so, pray and connect with God.

What are you sensing as you do this? What are you feeling?

How can making a few changes in your environment be a physical response to the spiritual truth that God is your true home?

Is there something you used to do that you want to begin again? (Exercising? Painting? Serving? Writing? Baking? Praying?) In the next few days, take a small step toward beginning again.

Pray

Read the prayer below or copy it in your journal. Add your own thoughts, experiences, and emotions as you write.

Dear God, I want you to be my true home. It's hard to see that all the time, when the temporal things of my life here on Earth feel like they are my home. But I know the truth. Every time you call me to begin again, like Abraham, I see and know that you are my truest home. Help me in the new things I'm facing, in the places where I feel like I don't see the next right step. Be near to me as I seek to be a woman set free, not only from bondage to sin but also from bondage to the things of my life today that may be keeping me from what you have for me. I am free in you; I am free with you; I am free because of you. Thank you for the freedom to begin again, in so many ways.

Free to Rest

We don't even know how to rest anymore.
CRAIG GROESCHEL

INTRODUCTION

The average adult needs 7.5 to 9 hours of sleep each night. I (Annie) do not know a lot of women who are getting that many hours on a regular basis. (Do you? If so, *tell me how to do it!*) Most single girls don't go to bed early enough, young mamas can hardly find sleep in general, and everybody has to wake up a few hours earlier than they wish they did.

But you have to get sleep. You cannot live without it.

Dramatic? Nope. It's the truth. In fact, four things are needed to survive (and, no, one of them is *not* coffee):

Air.

Food.

Water.

Sleep.

People don't talk much about sleep. When you think of necessities for life, food and water first come to mind. But you know from your own life, like I know from mine, that there are times when sleep is the only thing you need.

Of course, you can carve out all the hours you need every night for sleep and still not feel truly rested. While actual sleep surely helps, there is something deeper, isn't there? I think that's why David wrote in Psalm 62:1, "My soul finds rest in God." It's a different kind of rest—an internal, gut-level rest that doesn't have to do with actual hours of shut-eye.

Our Jewish friends call this intentional rest Shabbat or Sabbath. Once a week, from sundown Friday to sundown Saturday, they stop. They rest. They cease work and participate only in things that are restful or worshipful.

I once participated in a Shabbat meal while visiting Jerusalem, and it changed me forever. No phones, no technology, no cleaning, no cooking, no errands. Just quiet, peace, connection with God and people. The food was delicious (Israelis love love love hummus), more courses than I knew to prepare for! And we sat around in the family's dining room, sharing bread and meat and salad and soup and wine and stories for hours and hours. I never laid down once, but I felt more rested in my soul after that night than I had in a long time.

That kind of deep heart rest? It's what I crave. It's what freedom sounds like to me. I want to find it more and more in my life, as I abide in the Vine, as I draw near to God, as I confess and declare, as I rest.

Freedom is found in rest. Rest is found in freedom.

WELCOME

Welcome to the fourth session of You Are Free: Be Who You Already Are. *To get things started, go around the group and discuss any one of the following questions:*

- What insights do you have to share with the group from the between-sessions study last week?

- How many hours of sleep are you getting each night? Do you wish you were getting more? *6 - 6½   Yes!*
- If you got a day off to do whatever you wanted, and money was no object, how would you spend your day? What would you do to feel rested by the end of the day?

VIDEO PRESENTATION

Play the video segment for session four. As you watch, use the following outline to record any thoughts or concepts that stand out to you.

Notes

Runners don't want to rest.

Jesus says → just show up!!

Come →
abide →

Some principles and realities are so profound and life changing that if we instantly transfer them to somebody else, we actually don't get the benefit of whatever the revelation is that the Lord gave us.

Writing is a way to process your thoughts and take captive thoughts that wander. You know we're supposed to do that and not just let them spin out of control.

By getting some of your doubts, fears, and insecurities down, even in a journal, it allows the Lord to show you that you can release the power of the lies in your life.

The Word of God is living and active and able to play a role in your rest and freedom.

The nature of a natural vine in a vineyard is that anything it touches, anything it encounters, it begins to wrap itself around that item, that thing, that person, and make them one.

God will wrap Himself around me.

We don't have to put pressure on ourselves to know God more, serve him more, etc. Stop performing for love. Matt 11:28-30 msg.

"I came to carry you. I came to carry this relationship with you, actually. I came to take the pressure off. If you just come to me. There's one thing you need to do. Just come to me."

In that union the Vine will begin to wrap himself around you, and he will start to pull you close. It will be easy and light. We don't have to put all this pressure on ourselves to know God more, or to love him more, or to serve him more. ✳ ✴ ✦

Do I have places left to grieve? Something that deeply wounded or hurt me?

GROUP DISCUSSION

Take a few minutes with your group members to discuss what you just watched and explore these concepts in Scripture.

1. Read **2 Corinthians 10:5**. What does it look like for you to take every thought captive? What happens when your thoughts hold you captive instead?

2. How does taking your thoughts captive lead to more rest?

3. Read **Hebrews 4:12**. How alive and active is the Word of God in your life right now? Why did you answer as you did?

4. How is the power of the living Word of God bringing you peace?

5. Read **John 15:5**. What does it say to you about "rest" when Jesus talks about how he is the Vine and we are the branches?

6. How do you see rest and freedom working together?

7. In your life, how hard is rest to come by? How specifically might the other group members pray for you to experience true Sabbath-like rest?

INDIVIDUAL ACTIVITY

For this activity, each participant will need a note card and two or three green pipe cleaners.

Just as was discussed in the video, when a vine wraps itself around something, it holds that thing in place. Similarly, it is the Vine, Jesus, who holds us—his branches—and our concerns in his tight grip.

On the note card write two or three things that are concerning to you right now, things that you want Jesus to hold for you. Also, write your full name on that card. Then roll it up, with your words on the inside, and take those pipe cleaners, like vines, and wrap them tightly around the note card.

Keep this little visual in a place where you can see it for the rest of the study, remembering that you can rest because you are held.

CLOSING PRAYER

Have everyone in your group hold their "vine-twisted" cards as they silently lift a prayer to Jesus, the true Vine who holds them fast in his love. Then, without opening the cards, have the women trade and pray for another woman's card. No need to look at the words, just pray for the same rest and peace that each woman wants for herself.

RECOMMENDED READING

As you reflect on what God is teaching you through this session, review chapters 9–10 of the book *You Are Free* by Rebekah Lyons. In preparation for your next session, read chapters 11–12.

Between-Sessions Personal Study

SESSION 4

*Y*OU ARE INVITED TO further explore the material you've covered this week by engaging in any or all of the following between-sessions activities. *Be sure to read the reflection questions after each activity and make a few notes in your guide about the experience.* There will be a time for you to share these reflections at the beginning of the next session.

REFLECT

Copy **Matthew 11:28–30** from your Bible in the space below.

Here is *The Message* paraphrase of those same verses.

Are you tired? Worn out? Burned out on religion? Come to me. Get away with me and you'll recover your life. I'll show you how to take a real rest. Walk with me and work with me—watch how I do it. Learn the unforced rhythms of grace. I won't lay anything heavy or ill-fitting on you. Keep company with me and you'll learn to live freely and lightly.

What is your initial response to this Scripture?

Take a moment to reflect on each section of this passage and apply it to your life. (By the way, this is a great method to make reflecting on Scripture a regular part of your relationship with God. Just take a verse, split it up into phrases, and think on each one.)

"Are you tired? Worn out? Burned out on religion. Come to me.
Get away with me and you'll recover your life."

Is there an area of your life where you feel particularly worn out? Write a little about it.

When I read "get away," I think of a vacation. I've had a vacation like that—the kind where I go and unplug and check out, read great books, and eat great food, and by day six or seven, I can take a deep breath and feel like something on my insides has healed. It feels like my life has recovered. But we don't get to go on vacation every week.

So what does it look like to get away with God in the life you already have and find that kind of nourishing, healing rest?

"I'll show you how to take a real rest."

How does going to God, spending time with him, bring you rest?

Why do you think it says "real rest"?

"Walk with me and work with me—watch how I do it.
Learn the unforced rhythms of grace."

Is this the divine version of "Take Your Kid to Work Day"? Imagine walking daily with God, working with him, as Jesus talked about, and watching how he does life.

What do "forced" rhythms feel like and look like to you?

Conversely, what do you imagine unforced rhythms would feel like?

How can we connect with God in such a way that we are walking and working *with* him, not *against* him?

"I won't lay anything heavy or ill-fitting on you. Keep company with me and you'll learn to live freely and lightly."

This phrase stuck out to me. Nothing that God gives me will be heavy or ill-fitting. My life doesn't always feel that way, but I have to choose the truth: with God, I can learn to live freely and lightly.

What in your life feels "ill-fitting" right now?

How can you actually trust that living with God is a chance to live freely and lightly?

This Scripture is so rich, so much to think about and learn. Don't stop reflecting on it as it comes to your mind over the next few days. Come back to these pages and continue to add your thoughts, your reminders, your questions. Find rest here, in the tight grip of the vine of Christ, as you wrestle with the truth of these words.

"Rest time is not waste time. It is economy to gather fresh strength. . . . It is wisdom to take occasional furlough. In the long run, we shall do more by sometimes doing less."

CHARLES SPURGEON, *LECTURES TO MY STUDENTS*

CONFESS

Let's continue to use the words of *The Message* version of Matthew 11:28–30 to confess our struggles with rest. Perhaps you've had similar conversations with God before. If so, you're not alone.

"I'll show you how to take a real rest."

What is it that gets in the way of you taking a real rest? Family? Friends? Work? Netflix? What do you tend to distract yourself with, thinking it will give you rest, but it never does?

"Walk with me and work with me—watch how I do it. Learn the unforced rhythms of grace."

Confess where you have regularly marched to your own drumbeat rather than walked obediently in God's rhythms of grace. Ask God to show you the unforced rhythms of grace that he has for you.

"I won't lay anything heavy or ill-fitting on you. Keep company with me and you'll learn to live freely and lightly."

Declare, in your own words, how God is the God of living freely. Turn this phrase into a declaration of who he is, how he cares for you, and how he will bring freedom and light to your life.

RESPOND

In the space provided or in your journal, answer the following questions.

Write

Read the following Scripture or copy it in your journal.

Are you tired? Worn out? Burned out on religion? Come to me. Get away with me and you'll recover your life. I'll show you how to take a real rest. Walk with me and work with me—watch how I do it. Learn the unforced rhythms of grace. I won't lay anything heavy or ill-fitting on you. Keep company with me and you'll learn to live freely and lightly (Matthew 11:28–30 MSG).

Based on the reflection time this week, which of the phrases of this passage stands out to you? Write it here or circle it above.

Write a short response as to why that line is moving your heart today.

What would it look like for you to embrace rest for yourself? To find freedom in that rest?

Over the next week or so, memorize Matthew 11:28–30, either in *The Message* paraphrase or the Bible version you are using for personal study. Write the passage on a note card and carry it around with you, change your phone's home screen with these verses as the background, or write it over and over in your journal every day until the words are hidden in your heart. Taking your thoughts captive is a lot easier when you have truth in your mind to replace the lies.

Act

Look at your calendar. Can you find a date this month where you can disconnect from technology and let your mind and soul really rest? Or maybe three or four hours where you can get away with your Bible and journal and seek freedom and rest? Make space on your calendar. You'll be glad you did.

Pray

Read the prayer on the next page or copy it in your journal. Add your own thoughts, experiences, and emotions as you write.

Dear God, I need rest, the real rest you offer. I confess that I have run from rest at times and lost my way in busyness. Teach me the unforced rhythms of grace, that I might see you in my every day, in the fast and in the slow, and that I would model that grace to the people in my life. I want my life, for the rest of my days, to reflect that I am a woman of freedom and rest. Do that in me. Change me. Help me to embrace the discipline of rest.

Free to
Celebrate

*There will be almost an abundance in my life that could never have
been there or I would not have even known or appreciated, had I
not gone through that wilderness or that brokenness or that grief.*
REBEKAH LYONS

INTRODUCTION

My (Annie's) thirtieth birthday party was one of the greatest events of my life.

I didn't know what was in store. All I was told by my friends was to be ready for dinner at 6:00 p.m. Then I was scooped up right on time and taken to one of their homes.

There, gathered, were ten of my best girlfriends. Seated around a beautifully decorated table on the patio with twinkly lights strung above them, they sat smiling from ear to ear.

A delicious looking salad awaited each of us, and out of the kitchen onto the patio walked six of our guy friends—our waiters for the evening—ready to serve us drinks and dinner. One of my best friends, a professional photographer, quietly popped around the table taking pictures of every moment that he knew I wouldn't want to forget.

The men sang happy birthday (welcome to Nashville—it was beautiful with multiple harmonies) and the women said kind words about me. I placed my hand on my chest, barely able to breathe out of thankfulness, and with tears in my eyes, I told them this had far exceeded any dream of my heart, especially because I had only been in Nashville for two years at the time.

After dinner, people began to stream through the door. My sisters, friends from home, practically every person I had met in Nashville, gathered in the backyard. I couldn't stop smiling, or crying, or smiling and crying.

It all felt like too much, like God's kindness was far more than I deserved. And it was. Then too, I had spent a lot of time sowing into those friendships. Many coffee dates and lunch meetings and tears and stepping out of my comfort zone to make new friends when I moved to Nashville—all those seeds were blooming into a bouquet far more beautiful than I could fathom. God had done it, I knew he had; he is the one who waters and grows all things. But I was celebrating a harvest of friendships and joy that I could have never imagined when I was looking at the seeds of sacrifice that got me here.

Celebrating is natural when there is a harvest, but what about during the sowing season? Or the waiting season? Are you free to celebrate then too? Learning to celebrate, to find true joy no matter your circumstances, is to step into a level of freedom not everyone experiences. But what is found there, with God and through God, is worth it all.

WELCOME

Welcome to the fifth session of You Are Free: Be Who You Already Are. *To get things started, go around the group and discuss any one of the following questions:*

- What insights do you have to share with the group from the between-sessions study last week?
- Describe the best party you have ever attended. What was the occasion? Who was there? What did you eat? What was the décor?
- Have you thrown someone a surprise party before? If so, how did it go?

VIDEO PRESENTATION

Play the video segment for session five. As you watch, use the following outline to record any thoughts or concepts that stand out to you.

Notes

Moses felt weak even in the middle of his most important assignment from God, and he worried that his own doubt was greater than that assignment. Exodus

Moses believes his doubt is greater than God's assignment. Moses thought "You have got the wrong person!"
God was trying to make the point "Moses, I choose You!"

Weakness is the secret to strength.   *weakness is not the same as meekness. Weakness gives God the power to rise up.*

Christ's joy is, and can be, your strength (see Nehemiah 8:10). He didn't give us his strength; he walks with us, and when we abide in him and him in us, he *is* our strength.

"Do not grieve, for the joy of the Lord is your strength."

You can pray to God and ask him to restore the joy of your salvation (see Psalm 51:12). We bring to him our sadness, and he trades it for joy.

We aren't supposed to produce or create our own joy; he brings it to us.

When we draw close to him and when we are near to him, he is our joy and our strength.

God steps bring all our brokenness to me — I will restore it."

If you are numb to the lows, you are numb to the highs as well.

If you never felt sadness then you wouldn't understand what true joy felt like

Psalm 30:5

Because of the cross, we bring Jesus our fear and he gives us courage. We bring Jesus our defeat and he gives us victory. We bring our sadness and he gives us joy. We bring our weakness and he gives us strength. We bring our brokenness and grief and he gives comfort.

We can sit back and reflect on God's goodness, even in a season of drought or wilderness.

Joy is not the absence of darkness. Joy is the confidence that the darkness will lift.

GROUP DISCUSSION

Take a few minutes with your group members to discuss what you just watched and explore these concepts in Scripture.

1. Have you ever felt as if you were going to crack, like Rebekah did at the sink? Briefly describe what led to that moment.

2. How did you respond to that emotional situation? Who, if anyone, did you reach out to (family member, friend, pastor, or counselor)? Did you or didn't you sense God's presence at the time?

3. Read **2 Timothy 1:7**. (The ESV puts it this way: "For God gave us a spirit not of fear but of power and love and self-control.") How does this verse speak to such difficult and anxious times?

4. When is a time in your life that you felt full of joy?

5. When is a time that you felt more stress than joy?

6. Rebekah says "weakness is the secret to strength." Why do you think that is true?

7. Read **Psalm 126:5–6**. What do you think about these verses? What does it look like to sow in tears and reap in songs of joy? Can you offer a personal example?

8. How can you reflect on God's goodness even in a season of sowing or pain?

INDIVIDUAL ACTIVITY

For this activity, each participant will need three or four beans or seeds.

Pass out three or four beans or seeds to each woman in the group. Talk about what that seed would become if planted in the ground. Get descriptive: talk about the flowers, the leaves, the vines, the fruit or vegetable that would grow. Discuss what, in your lives, you feel that you have planted and are waiting to see grow. Encourage the women to take the seeds home and put them in a visible place for the next few weeks to remember God's faithfulness, even in the waiting.

CLOSING PRAYER

Invite the women in your group to share about what their seeds mean to them. Have them partner up and pray for each other in this season of sowing, believing God for what he will do in their lives, and asking him for more peace, freedom, and joy as they wait for the harvest of what they have sown in tears, time, and prayer.

RECOMMENDED READING

As you reflect on what God is teaching you through this session, review chapters 11–12 of the book *You Are Free* by Rebekah Lyons. In preparation for your next session, read chapters 13–15.

Between-Sessions Personal Study

SESSION 5

YOU ARE INVITED TO further explore the material you've covered this week by engaging in any or all of the following between-sessions activities. *Be sure to read the reflection questions after each activity and make a few notes in your guide about the experience.* There will be a time for you to share these reflections at the beginning of the next session.

REFLECT

Have you ever seen pecans harvested?

I (Annie) recently watched a video on Facebook of harvest season in South Georgia. A small yellow truck with two long parallel arms rolls up to a pecan tree. The farmer directs one of the arms to each side of the tree, grabs the tree, and shakes it. Shakes it like crazy. And then the pecans fall to the ground like rain.

The next machine pulls up, scoops the fallen nuts into a massive bin, and takes them to the pecan plant to be shelled, processed, and packaged—ready for our holiday pies and all sorts of other goodies.

The process is fascinating. The result is delicious. But it never ceases to amaze me how an entire tree grows from just one of those pecans and then turns around and produces a tree-shake worth of pecans for our enjoyment.

Seeds are amazing like that, aren't they? Maybe that's why God, continually through the Scriptures, takes us back to seasons, seeds, and trees. Nature reflects for us often in the physical what God wants us to understand in the spiritual.

I think God wants us to understand agriculture. I think he wants us to see that the thing you plant isn't what you get back—it grows into something different, something so much more. It multiplies and provides far more than what you planted in the first place.

Read **Psalm 126:5–6** again (you read it during the group discussion earlier). Does the analogy of the pecan harvest help you better understand the positive things that come from what feel like nothing-but-negative experiences?

How would you describe the difference between merely reaping in joy and reaping in "songs of joy"?

When we plant tears, what grows is joy. Songs of joy. That seems like a miracle. But then again, a pecan turning into a tree is kind of a miracle too, isn't it?

Harvest season is a time of celebration all across South Georgia as the pecan trees get all shook up and the hard work of a year of sowing and tending and caring turns into a plant full of nuts. Harvest parties are thrown to celebrate the bounty of the season.

There is a time to celebrate. After the sowing, after the care, after the waiting and after the harvest, you need to celebrate.

Read **Ecclesiastes 3** and match the pairs that are listed in the two columns below. (Note: These words are from the NIV version.)

born	hate
kill	mend
weep	give up
scatter stones	heal
war	gather them
tear	peace
keep	speak
search	throw away
love	die
mourn	laugh
embrace	dance
be silent	build
tear down	uproot
plant	refrain from embracing

Which pair stands out to you today? Why?

Do you see these things to be true in the world today? In what way(s)?

Which pair reminds you of what is going on in your family? Your church? Your job? Your country?

There is a time for everything—for the sowing *and* the reaping. The same is true in your journey with God. There is a time to mourn *and* a time to dance (Ecclesiastes 3:4). And there is freedom in the dancing, in the celebrating, in the pause from the work and waiting and just allowing yourself to celebrate. It's time to reap in joy.

 "Joy is not the absence of darkness. Joy is confidence that the darkness will lift."
YOU ARE FREE, PAGE 182

CONFESS

Often we want to rush the sowing season and hurry straight to the harvest, thinking the only time we can celebrate is when things have grown and are visible. But God has something specific for us in each season, and seeing it, celebrating it, confessing it, declaring it, and embracing it will open you up to more joy in the current seasons and freedom to live right where you are instead of wishing it away.

Read **1 Corinthians 3:6–9**. Who, according to the apostle Paul, did the spiritual planting among the Corinthians? And who did the watering?

Who made things grow?

Bonus question: Who did the harvesting?

Try to think of one area of your life that represents each season right now:

- Sowing/Planting = _____
- Waiting/Watering = _____
- Harvest = _____

We will take a little time to do some confessing and declaring around each season.

1. Sowing/Planting = _____

Why does sowing into this particular thing matter to you?

What do you hope to see grow from this effort?

What is there to celebrate right now in this story?

Confess to God your fears about what you are sowing into.

Declare, in your own words, that God is a God of seeds and a God of miracles.

2. Waiting/Watering = _____

What did you sow that you are now waiting to see become a harvest?

How long have you been waiting and what has been the hardest part about the wait?

What is there to celebrate right now in this story?

Confess to God your worries, fears, and concerns about how long you've waited and what will come of this.

Declare, in your own words, that God is your joy and that this season has purpose and meaning, for your good and God's glory.

3. Harvest = _____

What were the seeds you planted to get to this harvest? And how long ago did you plant them?

What does the work look like to harvest what God has grown?

What is there to celebrate right now in this story?

Confess to God your exhaustion with this process that makes it hard to jump into the harvest. Confess any concerns you have about the harvest looking different than you thought it would.

Declare, in your own words, that partnering with God is the greatest joy a human could have. Declare your intentions in this season to persevere, work hard, and be a part of the harvest of this story for the glory of God.

RESPOND

In the space provided or in your journal, answer the following questions.

Write

What is worth celebrating in your life right now? Try to think of at least five things.

1. _____
2. _____
3. _____
4. _____
5. _____

What seeds have you sown lately?

Read **Psalm 126:2–3** below or copy it in your journal. Then circle the word "joy" every time it appears. Draw a heart around each "The Lord." Underline "great things."

Our mouths were filled with laughter, our tongues with songs of joy. Then it was said among the nations, "The Lord has done great things for them." The Lord has done great things for us, and we are filled with joy.

What great things has the Lord done for you? Again, try to think of at least five things that he has done in the last five years.

1. _____
2. _____
3. _____
4. _____
5. _____

Act

Celebrate something today! Ask God to fill your heart with the joy of his salvation. And don't just celebrate in your mind; seriously throw a little (or big?) party. Bake a cake. Invite some friends over (or party alone, no judgment here). Get some confetti poppers from your local arts and crafts store. Throw. A. Party.

Why? Because God is faithful. Because we are free to celebrate anytime. Because we have confessed that God is a good God, One who always has something up his sleeve for us. Because whether we are sowing, waiting, or in the harvest, there is something worth celebrating.

Pray

Read the prayer below or copy it in your journal. Add your own thoughts, experiences, and emotions as you write.

Dear God, thank you for celebration, for joy, for the way freedom is so beautifully expressed in laughter and parties. Draw near to me in the seasons of sowing, speak loudly to my heart in the seasons where I am waiting for the seed to turn into something bigger and better, and give me the endurance to do the work required in the seasons of harvest. Be my joy. In all of it, help me reflect your goodness to the world around me.

Free to

Set Free

These things I know:
Freedom begets freedom.
Freedom is contagious.
Freedom frees us to set others free.
REBEKAH LYONS

INTRODUCTION

My (Annie's) friend Danielle Walker, better known as the author of *Against All Grain* cookbooks, blogger at againstallgrain.com, and @againstallgrain, has an autoimmune disease that has caused her a lot of pain, loss, trauma, and worry in the years since she was diagnosed.

From her website: "After being diagnosed with an autoimmune disease when she was 22 years old, Danielle realized that she needed to make dietary changes to end her suffering. She removed grains, lactose, and legumes from her diet, and started her blog to help others suffering from similar ailments continue to enjoy food."

What began as a blog, and experimenting with ingredients and recipes, has turned Danielle into a nationally and internationally known resource for clean eating.

Now her cookbooks are found in every bookstore and many of the chain stores. Every release hits the *New York Times* bestseller list. She travels around the country meeting men, women, and children whose diet and lives have been changed by her recipes. People who have felt trapped by their diseases or their allergies have been set free to enjoy food again.

You may not think dairy-free spinach artichoke dip has that kind of power, but trust me, it does.

It hasn't always been an easy road, but Danielle has fought for the life she has now. Danielle can invite other people into freedom because she has found freedom herself. Each recipe feels as if she is showing readers a place they will love but don't know yet. Like an explorer going on an expedition and then drawing a map for everyone else, Danielle has led the way, found freedom for herself, and now is spending her life inviting others to be free.

You can do that too. It may not be sharing the best recipe for dairy-free ranch or gluten-free buffalo chicken tenders, but there is freedom in you, waiting to be shared. And others will be set free.

For all the places you've fought for freedom, for all the seeds you've sown, for all the times you've chosen to celebrate, grieve, thirst, begin again, wait, ask—those same places where you have pursued and found freedom—those are the exact places where you can make a map for someone else to join you in freedom. Free to set free. That's you, friend.

WELCOME

Welcome to the final session of You Are Free: Be Who You Already Are. *To get things started, go around the group and discuss one or more of the following questions:*

- What insights do you have to share with the group from the between-sessions study last week?
- As our study comes to an end, what session stood out to you the most? What have you gained from this time together?
- What does it mean to be "free to set free"?

VIDEO PRESENTATION

Play the video segment for session six. As you watch, use the following outline to record any thoughts or concepts that stand out to you.

Notes

God speaks and things are created. *power of His breath & words.*

God will put the words in your mouth to speak to others.

Biblical examples {
Moses
Jeremiah
Isaiah 51

God chooses to let us be a vessel that he can use to declare his truth, to send a message, to wake us up, to remind us of things.

Jeremiah + Isaiah

What God said in the Old Testament about putting his words in our mouths, Jesus reinforced in the New Testament when he told how the Holy Spirit would be with us.

Holy Spirit will give recall of what God has said.

↳ Holy Spirit would help us even when we don't know what to say or pray.

You never arrive to where you don't need him desperately, daily, in everything that he asks you to do.

Love is a vital component to healing. *What does it mean to love in God's love and receive it?*

Rebekah: *"I don't know how to love."*

"I'm not worthy of love unless I earn it." Rebekah

"I'm not worthy of unconditional love"

"I'm not worthy of love if they're going to see all my junk."

We're supposed to sit in his presence and be filled by him as he gives us his love, like an outpouring.

Love is a healing balm that he floods into our hearts, and then it starts to play out in new ways of health, new ways of freedom and liberation.

If we could receive his peace, then we can offer that peace to others, and if we can receive his joy, we can start making other people laugh.

If we are open to him to come through us and pour out, we're going to love in a new way. We're going to love in an unconditional way and in a mighty way.

You alone were called to be free, but don't use your freedom to indulge your flesh; rather serve one another humbly, in love. Your freedom comes with responsibility.

Our calling is not for ourselves; it's for the good of others.

GROUP DISCUSSION

Take a few minutes with your group members to discuss what you just watched and explore these concepts in Scripture.

1. What are some things that people have spoken into your life that you have never forgotten?

2. Read **1 Corinthians 13** together from the NIV translation. Give your own one- or two-sentence definition of this type of love. Who do you know that loves really well, and what is one way he or she expresses it?

3. "Love is a vital component to healing." How does that phrase ring true for you?

4. How has being loved changed you?

5. Read **Galatians 5:1**. What are some of the ways we can stand firm and not be burdened by the yoke of slavery?

6. How have you personally invited others into freedom? Based on what you have learned in this study, in what other ways might you extend an invitation?

7. In what areas of your life do you still need freedom?

8. How are you different from when this study began?

INDIVIDUAL ACTIVITY

For this activity, each participant will need an 8½" x 11" piece of paper and some pens or markers.

We are going to create treasure maps to freedom.

Have each woman think of an area in her life where she has experienced freedom. Some examples may include: freedom from anger, racism, sexual sin, gossip, pain, illness, depression, gluttony, or heartbreak.

Have them draw that area as the start of the map and write FREEDOM on the opposite corner of the paper.

What did it take to get there? What people got involved? Add them to the map. What places did you go to—churches, meetings, rehab facilities, friends' homes, etc.—that helped lead you toward freedom? Add them to the map. When did you have a setback or a hard day? Add those to the map too. Include at least a half dozen spots on your map to go with your starting place and the destination of freedom. As you would see on any treasure map, draw a dotted line from start to finish, passing through all the points you have added.

When you are finished creating the maps, share them as a group. Have the women hold on to the map for this week's personal reflection and confession time.

CLOSING PRAYER

As this is your last time together, take a few minutes and share what you have learned about freedom over the past few weeks. Pray together, thanking God for these freedom maps, for these freedom weeks, and for all that is to come. Ask the women to share one area where they still would like to see more freedom in their lives and pray into that as well.

RECOMMENDED READING

As you reflect on what God is teaching you through this session, review chapters 13–15 of the book *You Are Free* by Rebekah Lyons.

Personal Study for the Coming Days

SESSION 6

YOU ARE INVITED TO further explore the material you've covered this week by engaging in any or all of the following between-sessions activities. *Be sure to read the reflection questions after each activity and make a few notes in your guide about the experience.* Try to meet with another group member in the days ahead to discuss this material.

REFLECT

I (Annie) remember the first time I had GPS in my car. As a woman who often gets lost, I had both car door pockets jammed full of maps that I used on a regular basis. But now, all that was solved by having a phone that could also give me directions. What a miracle.

It literally changed everything for me. Truly, I can drive with freedom now. I'm not worried about making the wrong turn or getting lost. I can't. As you probably know, when you make a wrong turn or miss your next direction, the app on your phone will correct and give you a new route.

That feels so much like God to me. When you are determined to follow him, when you want to live a life of freedom, when you are submitting yourself to his directions, you can't really make a wrong turn. Oh sure, you may miss a turn, but God will make it all work out. He will redirect you so you still arrive at freedom and get the chance to invite other people to join you.

Copy **Proverbs 3:5–6** in the space below.

What happens when you trust God?

How have you seen God direct your path so far in your life?

Look at the map you created in the group session time. (If you didn't do it, flip back for the directions and create a map to freedom.) On your map, take a green marker or pen and place a dot every time you feel like God stepped in and directed your path. What's the most significant green dot on your map? What did God do for you to direct your path?

Read **John 8:36**. "If Jesus has set you free, you are _____ _____." What does this mean about the end of your map? Draw a treasure chest at the end of your map and write "John 8:36" on it.

The creators of maps, the pioneers, don't just make maps for themselves, do they? No. The goal of a mapmaker is to create something that other people can follow, that will lead them to a destination.

What does it look like to share your freedom with others? Or to put it another way, how does your story, your map, make a way for your people to also be free?

If you were presenting your map to a room full of people, what are the three most important places you've drawn that you would share?

1. _____
2. _____
3. _____

Freedom isn't free; Christ paid it all for you. But freedom isn't only for you. We get to invite other people to live the free and abundant life with Jesus. *Is there someone you could call today to tell your story of freedom? Someone you would be willing to show your map of freedom?*

CONFESS

With your map in hand, and your study guide or journal nearby, let's look back at the last few weeks of study. Is there anything still gnawing at you? Anything you wish you would have dealt with that you didn't?

If the map is true for one area of your life, and God has a path for you to walk toward freedom, what does that mean for the other areas of your life where you are still struggling or desire deeper freedom and healing?

When you think of that, what area or areas come to mind? The chapters of the *You Are Free* book below may help spur your thinking.

1. To Be Free
2. Free to Be Rescued
3. Free to Be Called
4. Free to Confess
5. Free to Thirst
6. Free to Ask
7. Free to Begin Again
8. Free to Wait
9. Free to Rest
10. Free to Grieve
11. Free to Be Weak
12. Free to Celebrate
13. Free to Be Brave
14. Free to Love
15. Free to Set Free

Confess to God, in verbal prayer or in written form, that you still need freedom in some areas. Confess the worries or fears you have when it comes to inviting others to freedom and being a part of God setting people free.

On your map, draw a red cross in places where you had to confess fear, sin, or shame along the path toward freedom. How has confession grown as a discipline in your life in the last six weeks?

How do you see confession being a continual part of your life as you grow in freedom and grow closer to Christ?

Pick three points (at least) on your map that tell you something about God: his kindness, his love, his attention, his provision, his care, etc. Put a blue star at each of these three points and find a Scripture that speaks to that truth.

For example, if a conversation with a kind friend helped you take a step toward freedom, it might remind you of God's kindness. So at that spot, you would add a blue star and write a verse reference such as Romans 2:4 ("God's kindness is intended to lead you to repentance"). Use your Bible's concordance or the Internet or biblegateway.com to find verses you can use to declare God's presence on your journey.

Why does it matter to declare truth about God along your journey toward freedom?

Your map continues to develop, doesn't it? If you think of more stops along the way, add them! And remember, this is just *one* area of freedom in your life. You can do this for any freedom journey you choose to begin.

"You are invaluable to the kingdom of heaven. God has appointed a specific role only you can play. You are needed and wanted, chosen and set apart, beloved and worthy. You will receive all power and glory when the Spirit comes upon you. You will bear witness to everything Christ did to set you free."

YOU ARE FREE, PAGE 223

RESPOND

In the space provided or in your journal, answer the following questions.

Write

I (Annie) tape things into my journal all the time—sermon notes, a printed out devotional, a letter from a friend. If you can, take the map you created this week and either tape it in your journal or fold it up and place it there.

What emotions does this map unearth?

What are you most grateful for on the map?

What part of the trip did you enjoy the least?

How did God show up for you during this study?

Flip back and skim your "Respond" answers from the session one personal study (pages 30–31). Now reread **Matthew 20:29–34**, and then again answer the following question: If Jesus was standing right in front of you and he asked you the same question he asked the two blind men, how would you answer? What do you want him to do for you?

Act

Invite a friend to join you for coffee or lunch. Or ask your spouse to sit down with you for a bit. Tell the person about this study. Tell them about your map. Tell them about the new freedoms that you know and the areas in which you still want to be free. Be brave with the stories of your life and the past few weeks. Revelation 12:11 says we overcome by the blood of the Lamb (that's Jesus, and his work is done!) AND by the word of our testimony. Christ has set you free. Tell someone so they can find freedom too.

Pray

Read the prayer below or copy it in your journal. Add your own thoughts, experiences, and emotions as you write.

Dear God, thank you for freedom. Thank you for this study. Thank you for the ways you have shown up for me amid my sin and pain and anger and all the other emotions I have felt since we began. Seal the work you did here in my heart. Let the seeds I've sown toward a life of freedom grow into more than I could imagine. Allow me to be the kind of woman who is free to set others free.

Additional Resources for Group Leaders

*T*HANK YOU FOR YOUR willingness to lead a group through the *You Are Free* study. The rewards of being a leader are different from those of participating, and we hope you find your own walk with Jesus deepened by the experience. During this study, you will be helping your group members explore the Bible and find out what God says about experiencing the abundant and free life that he has in store for them. There are several elements in this leader's guide that will help you as you structure your study and reflection time, so take advantage of each one.

BEFORE YOU BEGIN

There are a few things that you will want to keep in mind before you begin the study. First, note that *You Are Free* is a six-session study built around video content and small-group interaction. That's where you come in. As the group leader, you are invited to see yourself as the host of a dinner party. Your job is to take care of your guests by managing all the behind-the-scenes details so that when everyone finally arrives, they can just enjoy each other.

As the group leader, your role is not to answer all the questions or reteach the content—the video, book, and study guide will do most of that work. Your job is to guide the experience and cultivate your small group into a kind of teaching community. This will make it a place to process, question, and reflect, not receive more instruction.

As such, make sure everyone in the group gets a copy of the study guide. Group members are free to write in their guide and bring it with them every week. This will keep everyone on the same page and help the process run more smoothly. Likewise, encourage the group to get a copy of the *You Are Free* book so they can complete the suggested readings should they so desire. Giving everyone access to the material will position this study to be as rewarding an experience as possible.

STRUCTURING THE MEETING TIME

You will need to determine with your group how long you want to meet each week so you can plan your time accordingly. Generally, most groups like to meet for either sixty minutes or ninety minutes, so you could use one of the following schedules:

SECTION	60 MINUTES	90 MINUTES
Welcome: Members arrive and get settled	5 minutes	5 minutes
Icebreaker: Discuss one or two of the opening questions with the group	10 minutes	15 minutes
Teaching: Watch the video	20 minutes	20 minutes
Discussion: Guide the group through the discussion questions	10 minutes	20 minutes
Activity: Do the closing individual activity	10 minutes	20 minutes
Prayer: Close with a time of prayer	5 minutes	10 minutes

As the group leader, it is up to you to manage the time and keep things moving along according to your schedule. You might want to set a timer for each segment so both you and the group members know when your time is up. (There are some good phone apps for timers that play a chime instead of a disruptive noise.) Don't feel pressured to cover every question or item if the group has a good discussion going.

ENVIRONMENT AND HOSPITALITY

As group leader, you'll want to create an environment conducive to sharing and learning. For this reason, a church sanctuary or formal classroom may not be ideal for this kind of meeting, as they can feel formal and less intimate. Wherever you choose, make sure there is enough comfortable seating for everyone and, if possible, arrange the seats in a semicircle so everyone can see the video easily. This will make the transition between the video and group conversation more efficient and natural.

Also, try to get to the meeting site early so you can greet participants as they arrive. Simple refreshments create a welcoming atmosphere and can be a wonderful addition to a group study evening. If you do serve food, try to take into account any food allergies or dietary restrictions your group may have. If you meet in a home, you will want to find out if the house has pets (in case there are any allergies) and even consider offering childcare to women with children who want to attend.

During your first meeting, plan to send a sheet around the room where the members can write down their name, phone number, and email address. This will make it easier for you to keep in touch with them during the week. Also, as you plan your meeting time, keep in mind that the ideal size for a group is eight to ten people, as this ensures everyone will have enough time to participate in discussions. If you have more people, you might want to break up the main group into smaller subgroups.

Encourage those who show up at the first meeting to commit to attending the duration of the study, as this will help group members get to know each other, create stability, and help you know how to prepare each week. Finally, be sure your media technology is working properly. Managing these details up front will make the rest of your group experience flow effectively and provide a welcoming space in which to engage the content of *You Are Free*.

STARTING THE GROUP MEETING

Once everyone has arrived, it will be time to begin the group. If you are new to small-group leading, what follows are some simple tips to make your group time healthy, enjoyable, and effective. First, consider beginning the meeting with a word of prayer, and remind the group members to silence and put away their mobile phones. This is a way to say "yes" to being present to each other and to God.

For the first session, ask one or both of the opening "icebreaker" questions found in the "Welcome" section. This will get everyone interacting and on the same page regarding the week's content. In future sessions, the group members will discuss what insights they learned from the between-session studies they completed during the week. Your job during this time will be to help the members "debrief" the previous week's experience.

This will be a bit different than the group discussion time, as the content will come from the participants' own lives. The basic experiences that you want the group to reflect on are:

- What was the best thing about the activity?
- What was the hardest thing?
- What did I learn about myself?
- What did I learn about God?

Remember that you do not need to be a biblical scholar to lead this or any discussion time effectively. Your role is only to open up conversation by using the instructions provided and inviting the group into the text.

EXPLORING THE TEACHING

Now that the group is fully engaged, it is time to watch the video. The content of each session in *You Are Free* is inspiring and challenging, so encourage the group members to take notes as they follow along with the teaching. During the group discussion that follows, encourage everyone in the group to participate, but make sure that if anyone does not want to share (especially as the questions become more personal), that individual knows she does not have to do so. As the discussion progresses, follow up with comments such as, "Tell me more about that" or "Why did you answer the way you did?" This will allow participants to deepen their reflections and will invite meaningful sharing in a nonthreatening way.

Once again, feel free to pick and choose the discussion questions based on either the needs of your group or how the conversation is flowing. Also, don't be afraid of silence. Offering a question and allowing up to thirty seconds of silence is okay. It allows people space to think about how they want to respond and also gives them time to do so. Once someone shares, you can then say, "Thank you. What about others? What comes to you when you think about this question?"

As group leader, you are the boundary keeper for your group. Do not let anyone (yourself included) dominate the group time. Keep an eye out for group members who might be tempted to "attack" folks they disagree with or try to "fix" those having struggles. These kinds of behaviors can derail a group's momentum, so they need to be shut down. Model active listening and encourage everyone in your group to do the same. This will make your group a safe space and foster the kind of community that God can use to change people.

CONCLUDING THE GROUP MEETING

The group discussion time leads to the final part of this study, the individual activity. During this section, participants are invited to transform what they have learned into practical action.

However, for this to be successful it will require some preparation on your part. Take time to read over each session's segment, as several of them require special materials. Reading ahead will allow you to ask group members to bring any items you might need but don't have, and will give you a sense of how to lead your group through these experiences. Use the supply list below to make sure you have what you need for each session.

Session One

- Note cards (one for each participant)
- Pens or pencils

Session Two

No supplies needed

Session Three

- Simple outline of a house—draw on a piece of paper and copy for each participant
- Pens or pencils

Session Four

- Note cards (one for each participant)
- Pens or pencils
- Green pipe cleaners (two or three for each participant)

Session Five

- Beans or seeds (three or four for each participant)

Session Six

- Paper (one 8 1/2" x 11" sheet for each participant)
- Pens or markers

As always, feel free to strike out on your own. Just make sure you do something intentional to mark the end of the meeting. It may also be helpful to take time before or after the closing prayer to go over that week's between-sessions personal activities, if time allows. This will allow people to ask any questions they have so everyone can depart in confidence.

Thank you again for taking the time to lead your group. May God reward your efforts and dedication and make your time together in *You Are Free* fruitful for his kingdom.

You Are Free

Be Who You Already Are

Rebekah Lyons

Have you bought the lie? Many of us do. We measure our worth by what others think of us. We compare and strive, existing mostly for the approval of others. Pressure rises, anxiety creeps in, and we hustle to keep up.

Jesus whispers, *I gave my life to set you free. I gave you purpose. I called you to live in freedom in that purpose.* Yet we still hobble through life, afraid to confess all the ways we push against this truth, because we can't even believe it. We continue to grasp for the approval of anyone that will offer it: whether strangers, friends, or community.

Christ doesn't say you *can* be or *may* be or *will* be free. He says you *are* free. Dare you believe it?

In *You Are Free*, Rebekah invites you to:

- Overcome the exhaustion of trying to meet the expectations of others and rest in the joy God's freedom brings.
- Release stress, anxiety, and worry to uncover the peace that comes from abiding in his presence.
- Find permission to grieve past experiences, confess areas of brokenness, and receive strength in your journey toward healing.
- Throw off self-condemnation, burn superficial masks, and step boldly into what our good God has for you.
- Discover the courage to begin again and use your newfound freedom to set others free.

Freedom is for everyone who wants it—the lost, the wounded, and those weary from all of the striving. It's for those who gave up trying years ago. It's for those angry and hurt, burnt by the Christian song and dance. You are the church, the people of God. You were meant to be free.

Available in stores and online!